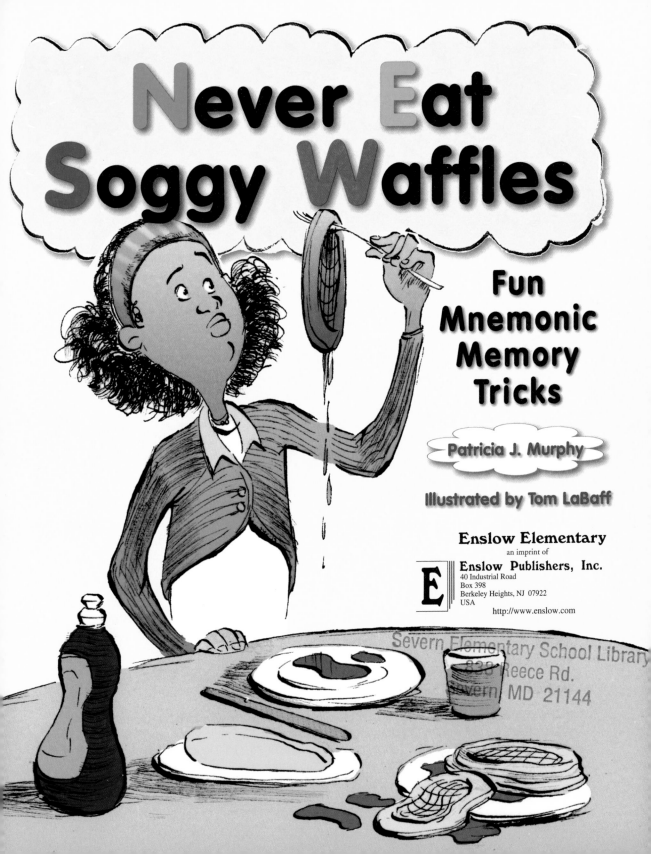

Never Eat Soggy Waffles

Fun Mnemonic Memory Tricks

Patricia J. Murphy

Illustrated by Tom LaBaff

Enslow Elementary

an imprint of

Enslow Publishers, Inc.
40 Industrial Road
Box 398
Berkeley Heights, NJ 07922
USA

http://www.enslow.com

In memory of my mother, Joanne O. Murphy

Library of Congress Cataloging-in-Publication Data

Murphy, Patricia J., 1963–
    Never eat soggy waffles : fun mnemonic memory tricks / by Patricia J. Murphy.
        p. cm.
    Summary: "Introduces young readers to the concept of mnemonic devices, presenting
        several examples of mnemonics as study aids and explaining how mnemonic devices
        are created"—Provided by publisher.
    Includes bibliographical references and index.
    ISBN 978-0-7660-2710-7
    1. Mnemonics—Juvenile literature. I. Title.
    BF385.M95 2008
    153.1'4—dc22

                                          2007044888

ISBN-10: 0-7660-2710-4

Printed in the United States of America

10 9 8 7 6 5 4 3 2

To Our Readers:
We have done our best to make sure all Internet Addresses in this book were active and appropriate when we went to press. However, the author and the publisher have no control over and assume no liability for the material available on those Internet sites or on other Web sites they may link to. Any comments or suggestions can be sent by e-mail to comments@enslow.com or to the address on the back cover.

♻ Enslow Publishers, Inc., is committed to printing our books on recycled paper. The paper in every book contains 10% to 30% post-consumer waste (PCW). The cover board on the outside of each book contains 100% PCW. Our goal is to do our part to help young people and the environment too!

Illustration Credits: Tom LaBaff

Photo Credits: Enslow Publishers, p. 18 (apatite, orthoclase); National Oceanic and Atmospheric Administration/Department of Commerce, p. 40; Shutterstock, pp. 5, 6, 18 (talc, gypsum, calcite, fluorite, quartz, topaz, corundum), 30, 31, 38; U.S. Department of Agriculture, p. 32; © Wilson Valentin/iStockphoto.com, p. 18 (diamond).

Cover Illustration: Tom LaBaff

Contents

Introduction: Everybody Forgets!

Quick! What did you have for breakfast last Tuesday? What was your second-grade teacher's last name? What are the names of the planets?

How did you do? Could you answer these questions? If yes, congratulations! If no, don't worry! You are not alone. The brain's memory center is one busy place. It is receiving, sorting, filing, and changing information all the time. Sometimes, the memory center slips up—and you forget.

It's a safe bet that you won't forget something that you've connected with a feeling (happiness) or special meaning (your mom's birthday!), or something you've practiced again and again (riding a bike). But other things will stay only a short time—and then move out.

As for REALLY LONG LISTS of things that you need to remember—like when you're learning something new or studying for a test—that's when a **mnemonic (nih MAH nik) device** can help.

Just What Is a Mnemonic Device?

Mnemonic devices are memory tools or aids that you can use to remember all sorts of things. Many of them work by using the first letter of each item in a list to create an easy-to-remember phrase. While using them cannot improve your memory or increase your brain's storage space, they *can* offer your memory unusual ways to remember information that you might not usually remember. Cool, huh?

How do you use them? It's easy. To remember the phases of the moon, just think **D O C.** The shapes of the letters match the shapes of the phases of the moon.

 The **D** represents the waxing moon.

 The **O** represents the full moon.

 The **C** represents the waning moon.

Why use them? Mnemonic devices are easier and a whole lot more fun to remember than the long lists of things that they represent. Really!

Who uses them? Smart people like YOU, scientists, mathematicians, musicians, doctors, lawyers, teachers, artists, and writers can and do use mnemonic devices.

What now? Turn the page to discover 19 mnemonic devices with over 100 memorable pieces of information that won't make your brain hurt. We promise!

When you want to remember:

The Cardinal Directions
(in clockwise order)

Think:

Never Eat Soggy Waffles!

North
East
South
West

N

W   E

S

Think:

Roy G. Biv

Red, Orange, Yellow, Green, Blue, Indigo, Violet

When you want to remember:

The Number of Days in Each Month

January: 31
February: 28 or 29
March: 31
April: 30
May: 31
June: 30
July: 31
August: 31
September: 30
October: 31
November: 30
December: 31

Try this:

Hold your fists side by side with your knuckles facing up. Start with the first knuckle on your left, and name each knuckle and "valley" (the space between each knuckle) a month of the year from January to December. Each knuckle stands for a month that has 31 days. Each valley stands for a month that has 30 days—except February, which has 28 or 29 days. This mnemonic device will come in handy when there's no calendar around!

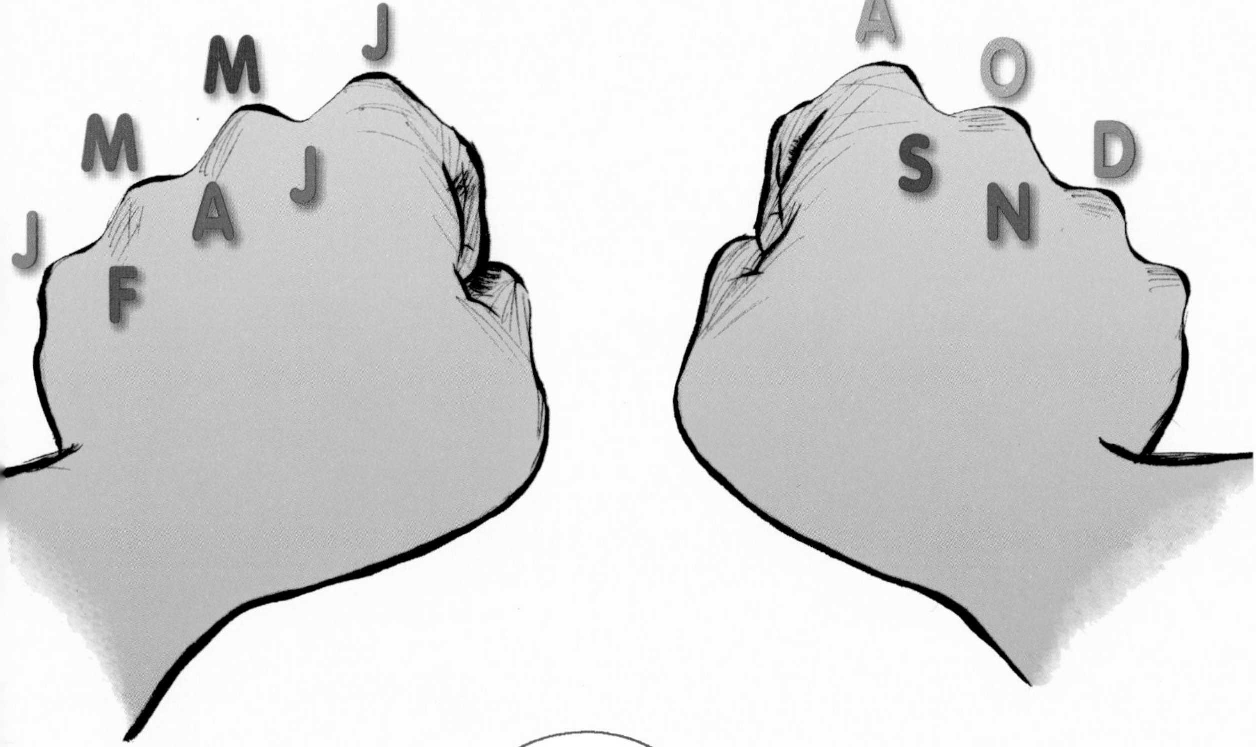

J
M
M
J
A
J
F

A
S
O
N
D

You can use this rhyme to
remember the days, too:
"Thirty days have September,
April, June, and November.
All the rest have 31,
except for February, which
has 28—and sometimes 29."

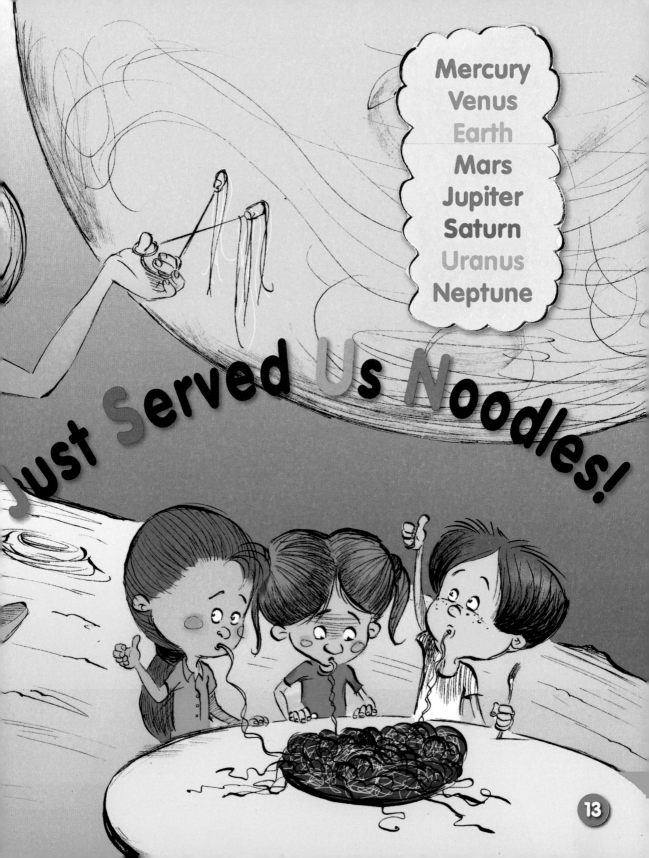

Huron, Ontario, Michigan, Erie, Superior

If you want to remember the Great Lakes from West to East, try this stinky mnemonic device:

Susie Made Henry Eat Onions.

Think:

I Am A Super Person

Indian, Atlantic, Arctic, Southern, Pacific

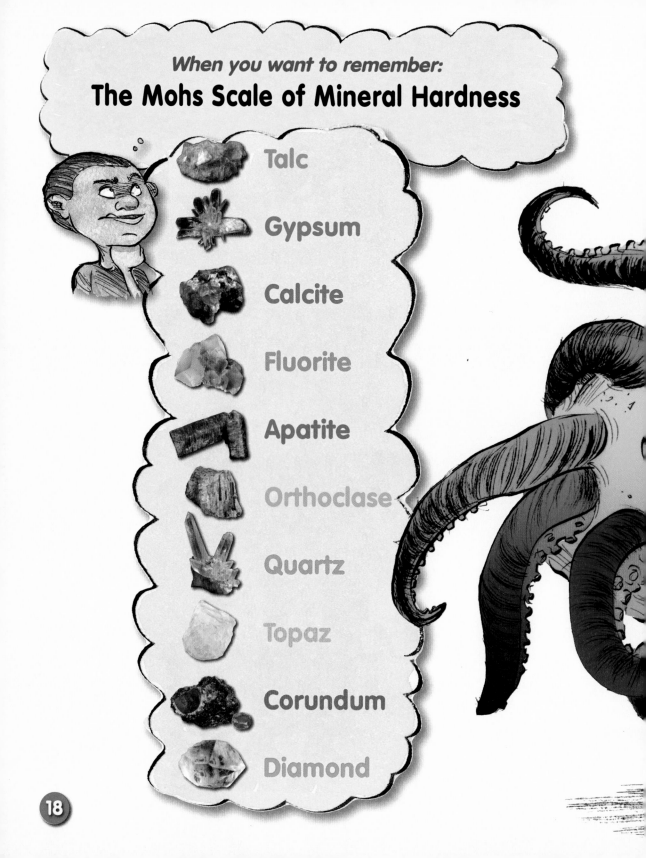

When you want to remember:

The Mohs Scale of Mineral Hardness

Talc

Gypsum

Calcite

Fluorite

Apatite

Orthoclase

Quartz

Topaz

Corundum

Diamond

Think:

The Good Cook Found An Octopus Quiche To Call Dinner

19

When you want to remember:
Earth's Land Biomes

Think:

The Dry Desert Grows Terrific Castles

Tundra, Deciduous Forest, Desert, Grassland, Tropical Rain Forest, Coniferous Forest

The Order of Math Operations

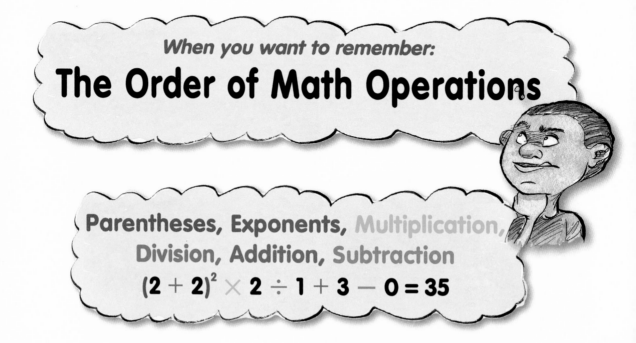

Parentheses, Exponents, Multiplication, Division, Addition, Subtraction

$$(2 + 2)^2 \times 2 \div 1 + 3 - 0 = 35$$

Think:

Please Excuse My Dear Aunt Sally

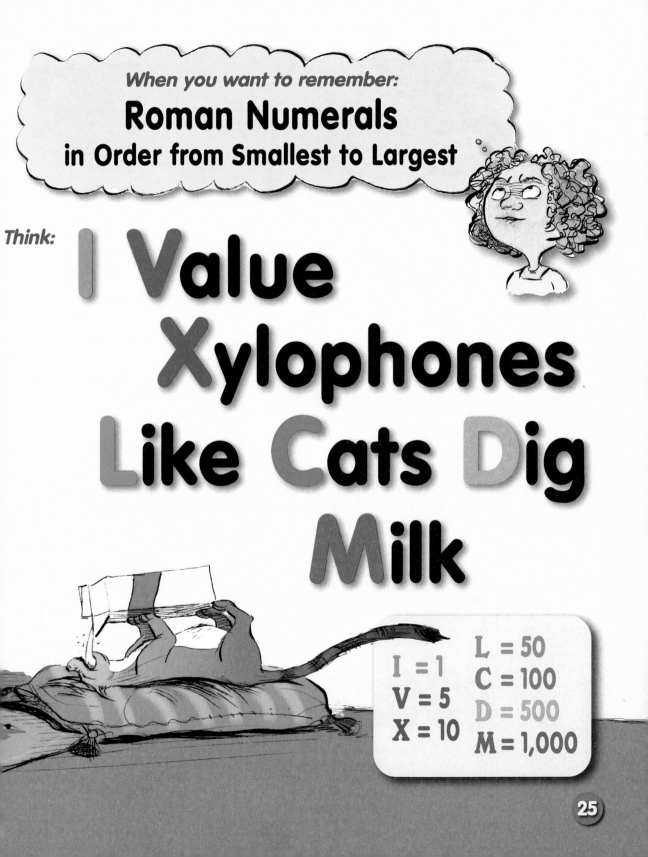

When you want to remember:

The Digits of Pi

Think:

How I Wish I Could Recollect Pi Easily Today

This mnemonic device works differently. The number of letters in each word of the device matches up to the first nine digits of pi.

π = 3.14159265

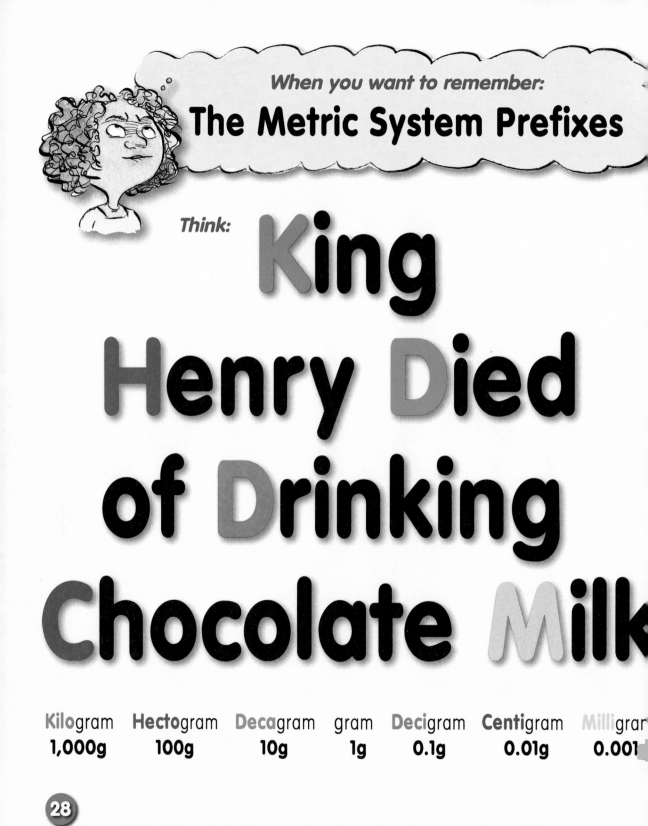

When you want to remember:

The Metric System Prefixes

Think:

King
Henry Died
of Drinking
Chocolate Milk

Kilogram	**Hecto**gram	**Deca**gram	gram	**Deci**gram	**Centi**gram	**Milli**gram
1,000g	100g	10g	1g	0.1g	0.01g	0.001

The **FACE** mnemonic device gives you the names of the notes that lie on the spaces of the treble clef, moving from bottom to top.

When you want to remember:

MyPyramid Groups

Think:

Giant Vinny's Flimsy Exercise Machine Might Break!

Grains, **Vegetables,** Fruits, **Exercise,** Milk, Meat, Beans

MyPyramid
STEPS TO A HEALTHIER YOU
MyPyramid.gov

GRAINS VEGETABLES FRUITS MILK MEAT & BEANS

MyPyramid is a guide to help you remember what to eat to be healthy. It also reminds you to exercise!

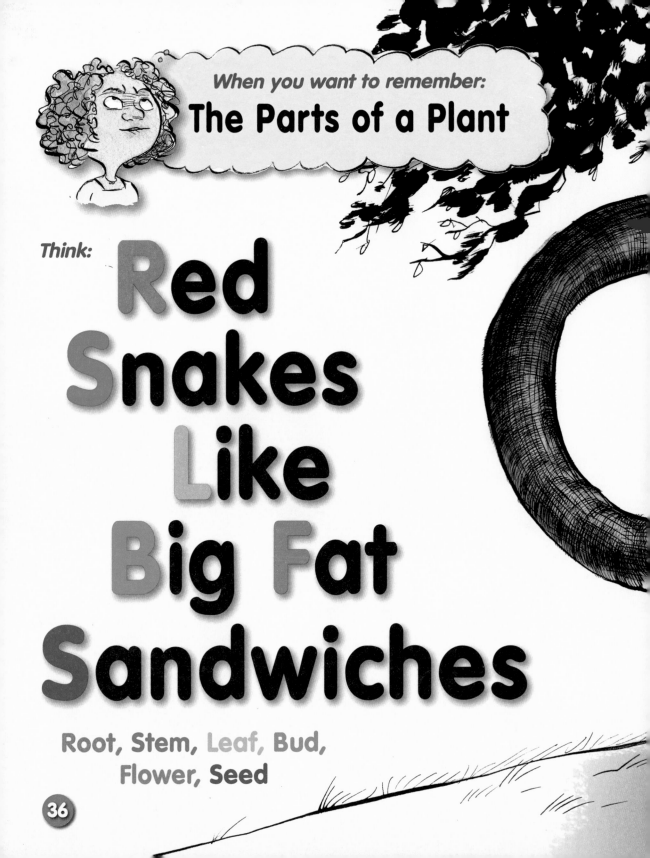

When you want to remember:
The Parts of a Plant

Think:

Red
Snakes
Like
Big Fat
Sandwiches

**Root, Stem, Leaf, Bud,
Flower, Seed**

bud—

— seed

— flower

— leaves

— stem

— root

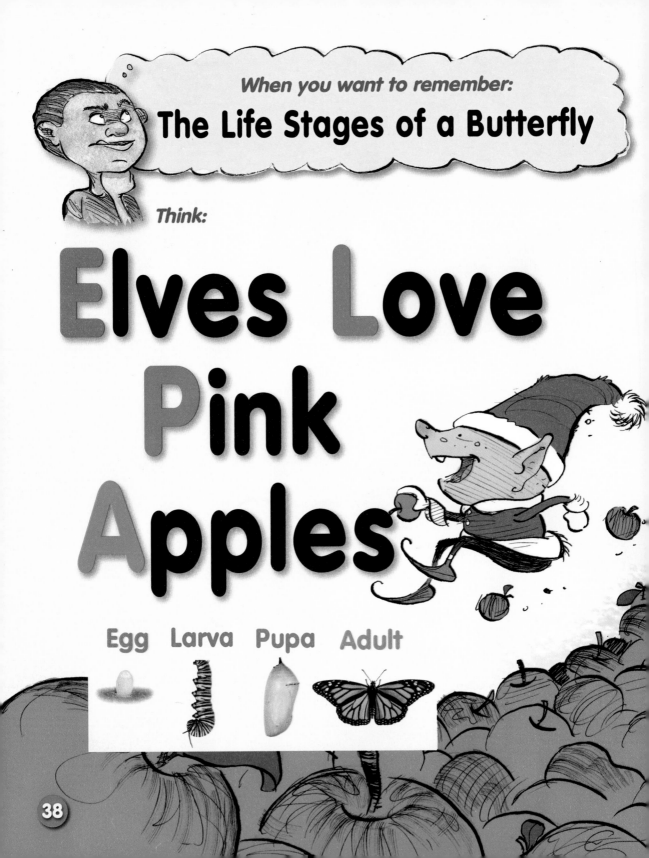

When you want to remember:

The Life Stages of a Butterfly

Think:

Elves Love Pink Apples

Egg Larva Pupa Adult

When you want to remember:

The Types of Clouds

Cirrus Cumulus **Stratus**

Think:

Cirrus clouds are high, wispy clouds made of ice crystals. Cumulus clouds are large and puffy. Stratus clouds are low and stretch out across the sky.

Cool Cats Sing!

When you want to remember:

The Body's Major Systems

Think:

Can Dad Eat Every Item In Mom's New Red Refrigerator? Sure!

Cardiovascular	Muscular
Digestive	Nervous
Endocrine	Reproductive
Excretory	Respiratory
Immune	Skeletal
Integumentary	

Make Your Own Mnemonic Devices

Now it's your turn. Use the steps below to make your own mnemonic devices. You can make them to remember spelling words, foreign words, long lists, test items, and more!

1. **Think**—What do you want to remember?

2. **Make a list**—List the things you need to remember in the order you need to remember them.

3. **Write it down**—Write down the first letter of each word in a column.

4. **Make it silly**—Make up a silly phrase or sentence using words that start with the letters on your list. Remember: The sillier or more meaningful this phrase is to you, the easier it will be to remember!

5. **Remember it**—Practice remembering that phrase when you want to remember the original list. Create an image in your mind to go with your phrase. Say it out loud, write it down, or act it out. Do whatever it takes.

Here's an example:

1. The order of rock, paper, scissors

2. **Rock, paper, scissors**

3. R
   P
   S

4. **R**owdy **P**eople **S**cream!

5. Picture people screaming during a rock, paper, scissors game!

Memorable Activities

Aside from mnemonic devices, there are other activities that can improve and protect your memory. Here are a few:

 1. **Chunk it**—Sort a large amount of information into smaller chunks or groups like you do with phone numbers.

 2. **Picture this**—Imagine what you want to remember, like a face or a name. Pair something about that person with the name that is memorable to you. If your new swimming coach is named Dotty, picture her wearing polka dots!

 3. **Rhyme time**—Use funny rhymes and phrases to remember things like, "I before E except after C."

4. **Map it**—Pair things you want to remember with places along your way to school. Through history, people have used locations to remember important points in speeches.

5. **Get organized**—Write down things that you want to remember (dates, things to do, grocery items). Put things away in the same place after you use them, such as your soccer ball or your library books.

 6. **Be safe**—Buckle up in cars and wear a helmet when riding your bike or skating. These simple acts can cut your chance of having a serious brain injury that could harm your memory for life.

 7. **Take care of your body**—Eat right, say no to drugs and alcohol, and get plenty of sleep and exercise. A healthy lifestyle can cut the chance of getting illnesses that might hurt your heart, your brain—and your memory.

8. **Tell a story**—Use a story to link all the things you need to remember. The memory loves a good story!

9. **Keep learning**—Learn something new every day! By doing this, you will keep your brain and memory healthy and active.

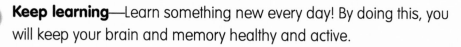

biome—A community of plants and animals that covers a large area.

cardinal—To be important.

metric system—The system of measurement used by scientists. Two basic units of the metric system are the **meter** (for length) and the **gram** (for weight).

Mohs Scale—A way of measuring the hardness of a mineral. Minerals with a higher number can scratch minerals with a lower number. The scale is named for German scientist Friedrich Mohs (1773–1839), who created it.

pi [π]—A Greek letter that represents the relationship of the distance around a circle (circumference) to the distance across it (diameter). It is equal to about 3.14159265.

scientific classification—The system used by scientists to sort living things into groups.

treble clef 𝄞—A symbol at the beginning of a musical staff that shows how high or low the notes on the staff should sound.

Memorable Books and Web Sites

Books

Brennan, Herbie. ***How to Remember Absolutely Everything.*** Harlow, England: Pearson Education, 2001.

McCrone, John. ***How the Brain Works.*** London: Dorling Kindersley, 2001.

Swanson, Diane. ***Hmm? The Most Interesting Book You'll Ever Read About Memory.*** Toronto: Kids Can Press, 2001.

Wilt Berry, Joy. ***A Book About Being Forgetful.*** New York: Scholastic, 2005.

Web Sites

Brains Rule
www.brainsrule.com

Exploratorium: Don't Forget! Playing Games With Memory
www.exploratorium.edu/memory/dont_forget/index.html

Kids Health
www.kidshealth.org/kid/htbw/brain.html

Index